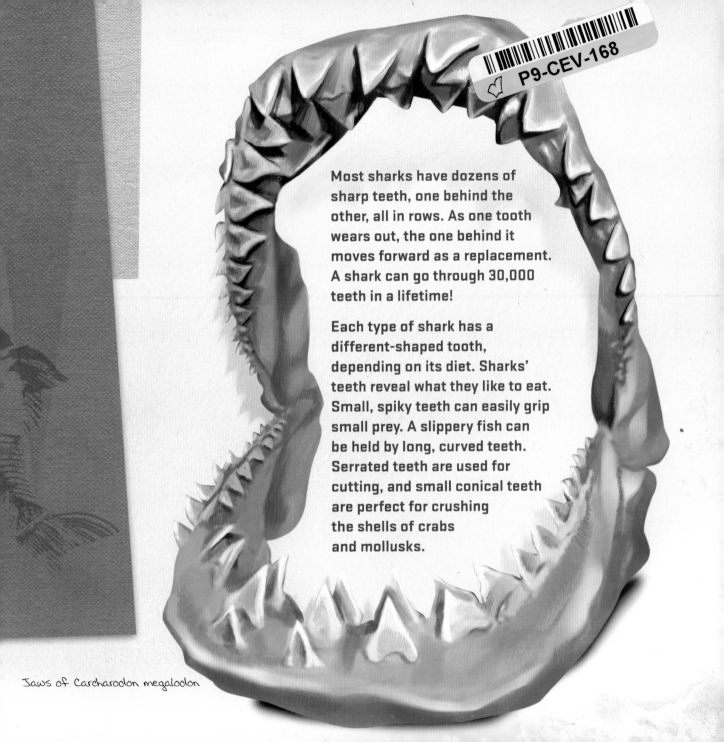

Most sharks have dozens of sharp teeth, one behind the other, all in rows. As one tooth wears out, the one behind it moves forward as a replacement. A shark can go through 30,000 teeth in a lifetime!

Each type of shark has a different-shaped tooth, depending on its diet. Sharks' teeth reveal what they like to eat. Small, spiky teeth can easily grip small prey. A slippery fish can be held by long, curved teeth. Serrated teeth are used for cutting, and small conical teeth are perfect for crushing the shells of crabs and mollusks.

Jaws of Carcharodon megalodon

HUNTING & FEEDING

Sharks are solitary animals. They live and hunt alone. Usually, sharks also eat alone, but sometimes one feeding shark will attract others. They swim toward a victim as quickly as possible and compete to get pieces of prey.

Great White Shark

SHARK BITES
A great white can go two months after a big meal before needing another one.

Almost all sharks are carnivores, or meat-eaters. They live on a diet of fish, sea mammals (such as dolphins and seals), turtles, and seagulls.

Not all sharks are fierce carnivores. Some of the largest—like the basking shark, the whale shark, and the megamouth shark—are harmless. These huge sharks eat plankton, a rich mixture of shrimp, very small fish, animal eggs, and larvae.

The most dangerous sharks to man are the great white, tiger, hammerhead, mako, and bull sharks. Most shark attacks occur in Australia, Brazil, California, Hawaii, Florida, and South Africa.

WARNING
SHARK INFESTED WATERS
SWIM AT YOUR OWN RISK

SHARK BITES
A shark's jaws are not connected to its skull, so they can open very wide for eating.

SHARK GALLERY

SHARK BITES
Hammerhead sharks love to eat stingrays. Scientists believe the hammerheads may have a natural immunity to the stings.

Whale Shark

The whale shark is the world's biggest fish. Even though it is called a "shark," this gentle giant is actually a fish. The whale shark can be up to 40 feet long and weigh as much as 20 tons.

Hammerhed Shark

Lantern Shark

The lantern shark actually glows in the dark! This bioluminescent, or light-emitting, shark is a bottom-dweller, living in deep waters where daylight doesn't penetrate.

Special light-producing organs, called photophores, produce a greenish light. This glow-in-the-dark effect is thought to help lantern sharks find mates and escape from predators.

Whale Shark

Hammerhead Shark

The hammerhead shark can be up to 20 feet long and is considered dangerous because of its size and predatory nature. The hammerhead shark's eyes and nostrils are set far apart, and its mallet-shaped head expands its range of senses.

Pygmy Shark

This is one of the smallest known sharks, measuring less than one foot. The pygmy lives in the depths of the sea by day and comes closer to the surface at night to hunt for squid, shrimp, and lanternfish.

Pygmy Shark

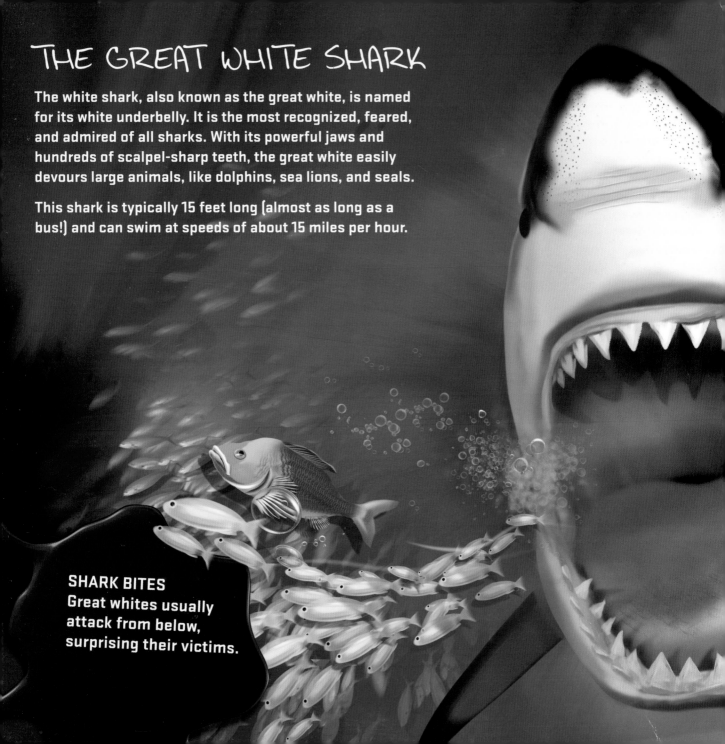

THE GREAT WHITE SHARK

The white shark, also known as the great white, is named for its white underbelly. It is the most recognized, feared, and admired of all sharks. With its powerful jaws and hundreds of scalpel-sharp teeth, the great white easily devours large animals, like dolphins, sea lions, and seals.

This shark is typically 15 feet long (almost as long as a bus!) and can swim at speeds of about 15 miles per hour.

SHARK BITES
Great whites usually attack from below, surprising their victims.

SHARKS

SHARK GALLERY

Mako Shark

The mako shark, which lives in tropical and temperate waters, is one of the world's fastest sharks, capable of reaching speeds of 20 mph. In fact, mako sharks and blue sharks are considered to be some of the fastest fish in any ocean. And if that weren't impressive enough, they can also leap out of the water!

Makos' tails are shaped like a tuna's. Active predators, they mostly hunt for schooling fish like tuna, mackerel, and swordfish.

Mako Shark

Tiger Shark

The tiger shark is one of the most feared sharks in the world because it is known to be a man-eater. It has a very large mouth with powerful jaws, and its triangular, notched, and serrated teeth can slice easily through prey. Most tiger sharks weigh around 1,400 pounds and are 14 feet long.

SHARK BITES
Tiger sharks can travel up to 50 miles a day.

Tiger Shark

Thresher Shark

Of all the sharks, thresher sharks have the longest tails; the upper lobes of their tails are about the same length as their bodies.

The thresher shark uses its tail to thresh (beat) the water when it finds a school of fish. This corrals the fish into a tight group, which makes it much easier for the thresher to stun and kill its prey.

Thresher Shark

Sawshark

The sawshark has a long, bladelike snout with tendrils on the side. The tendrils are used to slash at passing fish or to dislodge prey hiding in silt or sand. The sawshark's snout is also studded with sharp teeth.

Sawshark

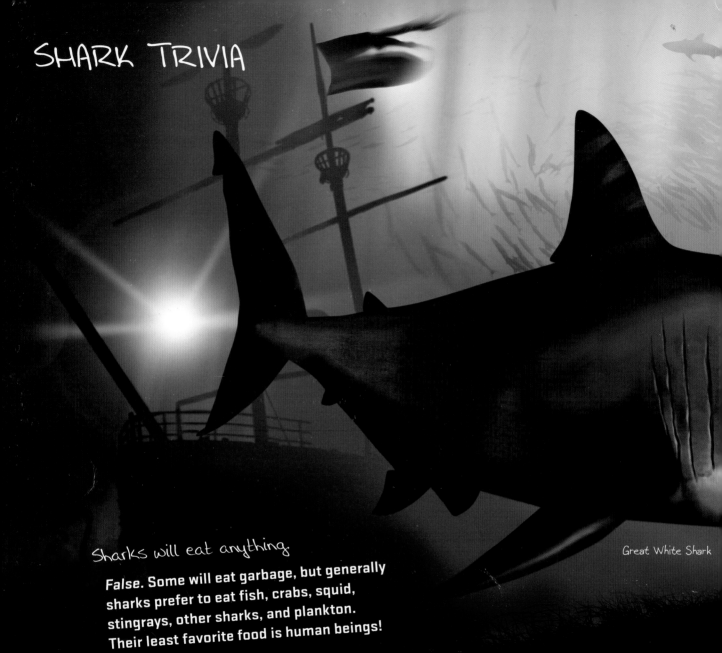

SHARK TRIVIA

Great White Shark

Sharks will eat anything.

False. Some will eat garbage, but generally sharks prefer to eat fish, crabs, squid, stingrays, other sharks, and plankton. Their least favorite food is human beings!